KU-732-316

Down on the Farm

DUCKS

Sally Morgan

QED Publishing

Copyright © QED Publishing 2007

First published in the UK in 2007 by
QED Publishing
A Quarto Group company
226 City Road
London EC1V 2TT
www.qed-publishing.co.uk

All rights reserved. No part of this publication
may be reproduced, stored in a retrieval system,
or transmitted in any form or by any means
electronic, mechanical, photocopying, recording
or otherwise, without the prior permission of the
publisher, nor be otherwise circulated in any form
of binding or cover other than that in which it is
published and without a similar condition being
imposed on the subsequent purchaser.

A catalogue record for this book is available
from the British Library.

ISBN 978 1 84538 808 9

Written by Sally Morgan
Designed by Tara Frese
Editor Corrine Ochiltree
Picture Researcher Nic Dean
Illustrations by Chris Davidson

Publisher Steve Evans
Creative Director Zeta Davies
Senior Editor Hannah Ray

Printed and bound in China

Picture credits

Key: t = top, b = bottom, c = centre,
l = left, r = right, FC = front cover, BC = back cover

Alamy /Renee Morris 5, /Arco Images 8, 9, 22, /Oote
Boe Photography 11, /Papilio 12 tl, /Chris George 16 tl,
/Beaconstox 19; **Ardea** /John Daniels title page, 10,
/Andy Teare 6; **Corbis** /Randy M. Ury FC, /A. Inden
15 ct, /Keren Su 16 br, /18 bl Reuters; **Ecoscene** Sally
Morgan 17 tr; **FLPA** /Flip De Nooyer/Foto Natural
5 bl, /Frank W. Lane 17 bl; **Getty Images** G. K.
Hart/Vikki Hart/The Image Bank BC, /altrendo
nature 4, /Dave King/Dorling Kindersley 12 br, /Luzia
Ellert/StockFood Creative 13, /Guy Edwardes/The
Image Bank 14, /www.korean-arts.com 18 tr;
Photolibrary Group Ltd 7

CONTENTS

Ducks on the farm   4

Ducks from *beak* to *tail*   6

It's a duck's life...   8

Dabbling ducks   10

Eggs and meat   12

Wonderfully warm   14

Different ducks   16

Duck customs   18

Quacking good fun   20

Glossary   22

Index   23

Ideas for teachers and parents   24

Words in **bold** can be found in the Glossary on page 22.

Ducks on the farm

Do you know where the soft feathers in a snuggly feather pillow and **duvet** come from? Many of these feathers come from ducks.

A mother duck swimming with her ducklings.

A group of Aylesbury ducks.

FARM FACT
Ducks can see almost all the way around them without having to turn their heads.

Ducks are found on farms all around the world. They are very useful birds. They give us meat, eggs and feathers. Ducks can help farmers, too. They gobble up lots of slugs and snails that like to eat the farmers' crops.

Ducks from beak to tail

The largest ducks can grow up to 40cm long, from shoulder to tail, and can weigh as much as 6kg. That's the same weight as six bags of sugar.

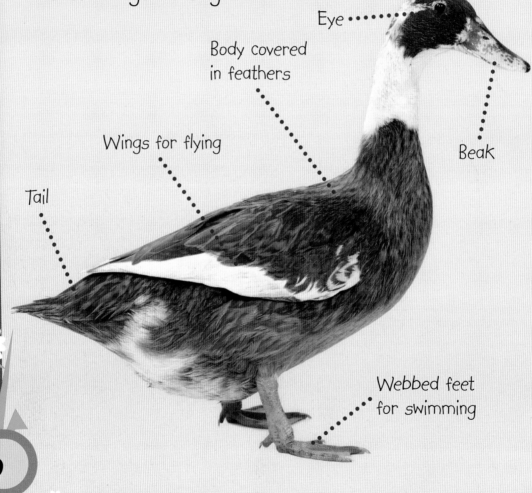

Eye

Body covered in feathers

Wings for flying

Beak

Tail

Webbed feet for swimming

This drake has curly tail feathers.

Height of six-year-old child

FARM FACT
Not all ducks quack! Only female ducks make a quacking sound. The drake makes a squeaky noise.

Male ducks are called **drakes**, female ducks are called ducks and baby ducks are called **ducklings**.

Height of duck

Some drakes are more colourful than ducks, and have curly feathers on their tails.

7

It's a duck's life...

A duck starts life inside an egg. The female duck lays eggs in a nest, then she sits on them to keep them warm.

The ducklings **hatch** after 28 days. Each duckling makes a hole in its shell with a special egg tooth at the end of its beak. It cracks open the shell and pushes itself out. A duckling can run around within minutes of hatching.

These newly hatched ducklings have fluffy feathers.

FARM FACT
Some ducks live for a long time. One white drake living in Wales reached the amazing age of 25!

Ducklings replace their fluffy feathers with stiff adult feathers when they grow up.

A baby duck has all its grown-up feathers by the time it is about seven weeks old.

A female duck starts to lay eggs during her first spring. Ducks can live for between two and 15 years, depending on how many eggs they lay.

Dabbling ducks

Ducks like to play in mud and make a mess! They push their beaks into the mud to look for small animals to eat, such as worms and snails.

Ducks also love swimming. They have large **webbed** feet that are perfect for paddling around in water.

Ducks cannot feel the cold through their feet.

FARM FACT
Ducks clean and comb their feathers with their beak. This is called **preening**. They rub oil, which comes from a **gland** near their tails, over their bodies to keep their feathers dry in water.

Sometimes a duck bobs up and down on the water with its head under the surface and its tail in the air. This is called **dabbling**.

A duck dabbles so that its head can reach the bottom of the pond to look for food.

11

Eggs and meat

Female ducks lay large white eggs. They are about twice the size of hen eggs. Most ducks lay their eggs during spring and summer, although some lay eggs all year round.

A good egg-laying duck may lay more than 300 eggs in a year! Duck eggs can be eaten, just like hen eggs.

Duck eggs can be used to make yummy cakes.

Duck is popular in Chinese cooking.

FARM FACT
The number of eggs a duck lays depends on the amount of daylight the duck gets. The more daylight – the more eggs!

Some types of duck grow very large, such as the Aylesbury and Peking ducks. These ducks are kept for meat in special farms. There are lots of these farms in South-East Asia and China. These ducks grow quickly and can get very fat!

13

Wonderfully warm

A mallard drake in flight.

A duck has different types of feathers. It has a layer of smooth feathers that covers its body. The long feathers on its wings are called flight feathers. They help a duck to fly. Small fluffy feathers called down feathers lie next to a duck's skin.

An eiderdown is a type of duvet filled with down feathers. It is named after the Eider duck.

FARM FACT
A mallard duck can take off almost **vertically** (upwards) from water. This means that it can fly over any trees growing beside the water without hitting them.

The Eider is a wild duck that lives in cold places where temperatures fall below freezing. It has very, very warm feathers!

15

Different ducks

INDIAN RUNNER
This is a tall duck that stands very upright. It is nicknamed the 'penguin duck' because it stands a bit like a penguin.

MAYA
The Maya duck comes from China. Flocks of Maya ducks are herded onto fields of rice. The ducks feed on insects and other small animals living around the rice, to help protect the crops from harm.

16

MAGPIE DUCK

This duck has white feathers with blue-grey patches on its head and body. It lays blue eggs.

CRESTED DUCK

The **crested** duck has a puff of feathers that sticks up on its head. Some look like they are wearing little hats! Crested ducks come in different colours.

17

Duck customs

KOREA

It is a **tradition** in Korea to give a pair of **carved** ducks as a wedding present for good luck. If the married couple is happy, they place the ducks so they face each other. If they are unhappy, the ducks look away from each other.

SINGAPORE

Many people around the world hold duck races. In Singapore, plastic ducks are let go on a river and float **downstream**. The owner of the duck that crosses the finishing line first wins a prize.

CHINA

Each autumn, Chinese people celebrate the Moon Festival. It is traditional to eat Moon Cakes during the festival. There are different types of Moon Cakes, but one type has a cooked duck egg yolk inside. People eat the cakes at night, under a full moon.

Quacking good fun

Make your own colourful duck. You will need a paper plate, an A4 sheet of yellow paper, an A4 sheet of orange card, pencil, paints, paintbrush, scissors, glue, feathers (optional) and a black pen.

1 Paint one side of the paper plate yellow and fold it in half. The yellow colour should be on the outside. Press firmly along the fold.

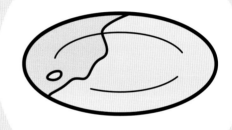

2 Place the sheet of yellow paper on a table and trace around your hand twice with a pencil.

3 Ask a grown-up to cut out the two hand shapes. These shapes form the tail feathers. Glue them into position on each side of the plate.

4 Draw a beak and legs with webbed feet on the orange card. Ask a grown-up to cut them out for you. Glue the beak and the legs to the plate.

5 Paint wings on both sides of the plate. Stick any feathers you have onto the wings. Draw on two eyes with black pen.

Glossary and Index

carved   shaped by cutting with a knife or sharp blade

crest   feathers that stick up on the head of a duck

dabbling   when ducks push their beaks into mud under water to look for food

downstream   the direction in which the water in a river or stream flows

drake   a male duck

duckling   a baby duck

duvet   a large bed cover, filled with feathers, that keeps you warm at night

gland   part of a duck's body that makes special oil which the duck uses to make its feathers waterproof

hatch   when a duckling breaks out of its egg

preening   when a duck cleans its feathers with its beak

tradition   a custom or way of doing something that is passed from parent to child

vertically   straight up or down

webbed   joined by pieces of skin, that make it easy to swim

Aylesbury ducks 5, 13

baby ducks 4, 7, 8–9
beaks 6, 10

cakes 12, 19
carved 18, 22
China 16, 19
crested 17, 22
customs 18–19

dabbling 11, 22
down feathers 14
downstream 18, 22
drakes 7, 9, 14, 22
duck races 18
ducklings 4, 7, 8–9, 22
duvet 4, 15, 22

eggs 5, 8, 9, 12, 13
Eider duck 15
eiderdown 15

feathers 4, 5, 6, 11, 14–15, 17
feathers, drakes 7
feathers, ducklings 8, 9
female ducks 7, 8, 9, 12
flight feathers 14
food for ducks 5, 10, 11, 16
food from ducks 5, 12–13

gland 11, 22

hatch 8, 22

Indian Runner ducks 16

Korea 18

Magpie ducks 17
mallard ducks 14, 15

Maya ducks 16
meat 5, 13
Moon cakes 19

Peking ducks 13
'penguin ducks' 16
preening 11

quack 7

Singapore 18
slugs 5
snails 5, 10

traditions 18–19, 22

vertical 22
vertical take-off 15

webbed feet 6, 10, 22
wings 6, 14
worms 10

Ideas for teachers and parents

- Read about the different breeds of duck. Make factsheets about the children's favourite breeds. Find out which ones are used for meat and which ones are kept for eggs.

- Visit a waterfowl or poultry centre where children can see different breeds of duck. A good time to visit is late spring or early summer when there will be ducklings as well as adult ducks. Some centres allow children to go into the incubator rooms to see ducklings hatch.

- Visit local ponds with the children to see wild ducks.

- Have a look inside a pillow containing feathers. Take one of the feathers and look at how it is constructed. Puff up the duck-down pillow or duvet to show how duvets and pillows trap air and help keep you warm.

- Make a collage of a duck. Take a large piece of white paper and draw the outline of a duck on it. Look through old magazines and cut out any pictures of ducks, ducklings and feathers. Collect scraps of material and natural or artificial feathers. Stick these onto the outline to make a colourful duck.

- Make a wordsearch using the duck-related vocabulary in this book.

- Compare duck eggs with hen eggs. Duck eggs can be bought in some supermarkets or from farm shops. Weigh a duck egg. See how easy it is to break the egg open. Compare the weight and ease of breaking with a hen egg. Make two lots of scrambled eggs, one with duck eggs and one with hen eggs. Ask the children if they can taste any difference.

- Ask the children to think of the names of famous ducks that appear in books, poems and cartoons, for example Jemima Puddle-duck or Donald Duck. Encourage them to write a poem about a duck.

PLEASE NOTE

• Check that each child does not have an egg intolerance before carrying out the scrambled egg activity above.